Pieces of My Heart

Poems and Quilts

Leslie Simon

AuthorHouse™
1663 Liberty Drive
Bloomington, IN 47403
www.authorhouse.com
Phone: 1 (833) 262-8899

This book is printed on acid-free paper.

ISBN: 978-1-6655-0125-5 (hc)
ISBN: 978-1-6655-0124-8 (e)

Print information available on the last page.

Published by AuthorHouse 10/07/2020

author HOUSE

Pieces of My Heart

Poems and Quilts

Leslie Simon

Table of Contents

Pieces of My Heart
Foreword

Pieces of My Heart is a unique mingling of passions – poems and quilts. Poems that express the author's laments and joys, sorrows and successes, worries and victories, these poems stand alone to welcome the reader in, share a landscape of emotions that do not wallow but search for a glimmer of hope through the darkest of tunnels.

These poems invite handmade quilts to join them, add vibrant dimension to words threaded stitch by stitch to build days past and pathways sewn together for bright tomorrows. Poems and quilts, words and swirls of colors, letter by stitch by verse by fabric, *Pieces of My Heart* engage the reader to immerse in words and pictures, a journey of heart that leads each one of us to today.

The message throughout *Pieces of My Heart* is healing. Body, soul, mind, repairing the past, patching tears in relationships, building traditions. You'll find these scattered throughout, "in the mirror of my life," "I am rubbed raw of thoughts," "dawn draws me to it," and "I am not present."

Darkness to light, "everything exists / to quiet a healing soul," and the past speaking through the author "centuries of people left footprints on the sand / for her to follow," "drowning in awareness of her consciousness," "helping me keep family traditions to pass on," and in retribution "in time you will feel the fire you set."

Joys and sorrows that flow "tears escape from my eyes / without my consent," and a view to the future "seven healing hearts to soothe a vacant soul." Here is your invitation to join hands with the author and stroll through *Pieces of My Heart,* "my heart's dream fulfilled / a life blessed / sewn into a mosaic of splendid pieces."

You'll be changed forever by the turn of each page, each poem and quilt binding you to this wonderful life. ~Judy Turek

Pieces of My Heart
Introduction

What is a poem? It's a quilt you wrap around yourself for comfort.

My poetry book connects the art forms of quilting and poetry. Cloth and needle...paper and pen, together tell a story. Quilts are sewn from scraps of cloth and poems from words, but both come from the heart to create a powerful image that touch emotions. For this book I've sewn a quilt to illustrate each poem, to bond words with thread, poem and quilt.

Years ago I started writing poems to release profound pain having been separated from people I loved. Writing poems was cathartic and helped me recover from an extraordinarily dark time.

Those early poems couldn't be written today. I am grateful that some of the people I lost returned to me...my life has moved on.

This book is my story.

In the quilt of life, friends are the stitches that hold it together. I am forever indebted to my lifelong friends who held me together.

Leslie Simon

Pieces of My Heart
Thank You

My journey began with Ellen Silverstein from my writing group. She invited me to a poetry workshop led by Gladys Henderson, the Poet Laureate of Suffolk County in New York. Gladys, an inspiration to the poetry community, made me feel valued and considered me a poet. I am so grateful to her for starting me on this path.

Phyllis Colby, an important forever person in my life, for giving me the idea and persuasion to publish a book of poems and quilts.

I could not have succeeded without my lifelong friends Marian Feliney and Nancy Wallach. Nancy, my book designer and proofreader...Marian, my partner in choosing fabrics and styling the quilts. They and my cousin, Ingrid Hirschbach (my lifetime consigliere) guided me through the whole process. Their enthusiasm overwhelms me with gratitude, their persistence motivated me to persevere.

Thank you, Barbara Dreyfus for sharing your grandmother's photo and to the ladies at Setauket Meadows for cheering me on.

My dear appreciation for my daughter, Jessica Zabell, for her enthusiasm and for never doubting my ability. I am in awe of her...she's an exceptional wife, mother, daughter and Earth Science teacher. Because of her I wanted to write this book.

The most important person in my life is my very own personal advocate, Anthony Forte, my husband, for encouraging me, giving me advice and converting the guest room into a sewing room for me to work on my project. I now have my dream studio. He's a man of many talents, I treasure him!

Pieces of My Heart
More Thanks...

Judy Turek...A chance meeting on the phone started a professional collaboration and friendship. She called to tell me one of my poems was being published, and we just hit it off. She is my editor and mentor. She helped me in all aspects of the creative process. Author of five full-length poetry collections, Long Island Poet of the Year and more than 23 years of devotion to the poetry community. She is known for writing a poem a day! She was enthusiastic about my project from our first meeting. We shared the same vision for writing a unique poetry book that featured quilts. I am grateful for her editing and guidance. At the end of the day, I'm most grateful for her friendship.

Roberta Leonard...Another person I was meant to meet. Sitting next to her at a meeting, I noticed her amazing handmade purse and commented on it. She told me she made it and that's how our relationship began. Roberta is my finishing quilter. She is a master quilter and winner of endless ribbons. I am totally entranced by her artistic brilliance. She is my inspiration.

Joseph Dlhopolsky...The photographer who did the most incredible job of highlighting the stitching details of the quilts. He's a lifelong Long Island-based photographer. His photographs have won awards and have been published in print media. Other examples of his work are on http://photo.joedlh.net. He is also a writer and expects before the end of 2020 to release on Amazon the third volume of his *Being Small* trilogy. He photographed and designed the cover of *Pieces of my Heart*.

Daniel Zabell...I'm so grateful to my brilliant son-in-law for spending so much of his time editing my poems, inspiring me to read them in the workshops and giving me confidence as a poet. His insight and expertise helped me focus on the intent of my writing and always found just the right word to express a thought. I respect his opinion and the fact that he liked my poems, means everything to me. He is an educator and my go-to person for all things poetic.

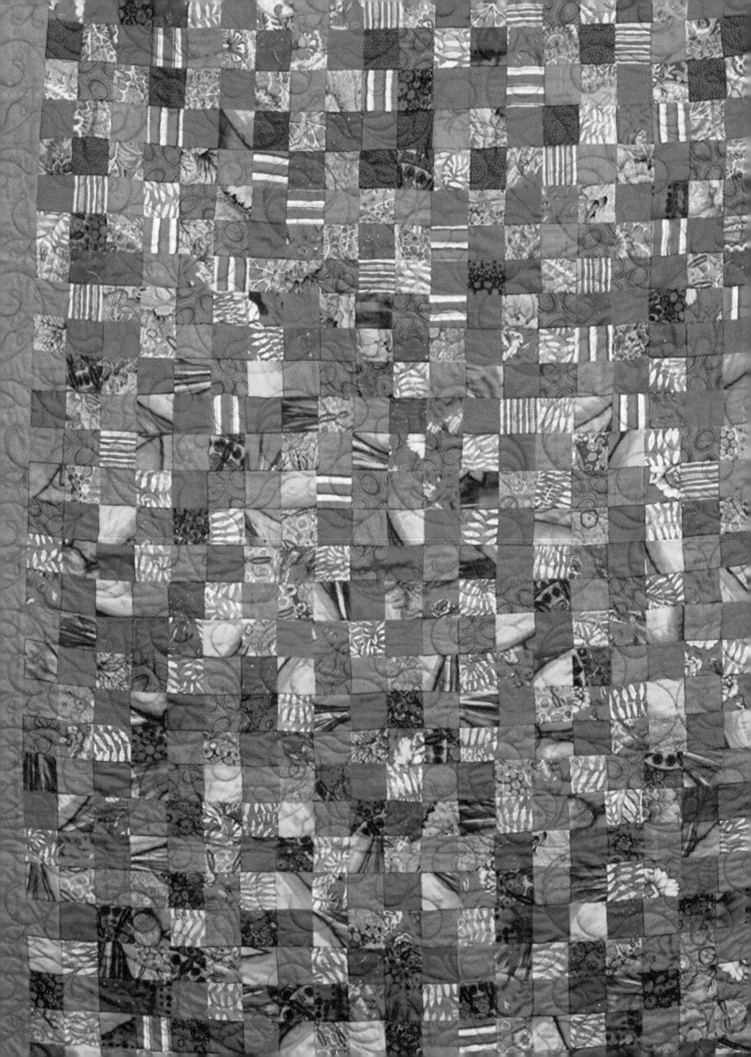

Pieces of My Heart
Dedication

To my husband Anthony Forte for bringing joy to
my life and to my daughters Jessica Zabell, Danielle
Fumagalli and Nicole Arnold who brighten my world

Pieces of My Heart

"I shall never get you put together entirely, pieced, glued, and properly jointed"

Sylvia Plath "The Colossus"

Sorrow

Drowning in Words

hateful words weighed me down
a cold heart watched as I sank

I waded in the safety of shallow depths
deep in panic, fearful of drowning words
I stayed away in denial

you knew I couldn't swim
I had no rescue line to save me
no way to stay afloat

flailing beneath to find breath
hands tried to reach me
I was too far under

above me others swam
I marveled as I watched their strokes
skimming water in grace and strength

screaming waves deafened your words
acceptance pushed me forward
beyond fear, rage took its place
I floated in defiance

Sadness Speaks

since she was born, we shared our souls
a small child looking for love

I have to imagine how she's grown up
and I wonder...does she ever think of me?

sadness has a voice
it speaks to me when I am silent

she is gone from me

I look at the moon, long for her
hear a song, her voice singing

no sunset happens without her next to me
no flower grows that isn't pink

alone, I planted our garden
waiting...but she didn't come

she is gone from me

I look for her everywhere
streets in town
at the beach
at all our places...always her hand holding mine

tears escape from my eyes
without my consent

she is gone from me

she is my sun, my light
I fear dark clouds approaching

You're Vile

You're vile, you make acid burn
You turn wind into deadly hurricanes

You scorch down trees
And close the light

You live in darkness
Where hate grows like fungus

You are...the mold, the germ

The parasite that eats away at the living
You are EVIL...a disgrace

I Am on Fire!

I am on fire
you've thrown coal into my heart
your words strike a match

my heart has been scorched
blackened by hate
burning in pain

rage buried under ashes is ablaze
bellows push breath into my core
flames' fury ignite strength in me

wind stokes the fire
sings a song of repair
sets my intensions

you will have to pay
for the destruction
in time, you will feel the fire you set

damn you!

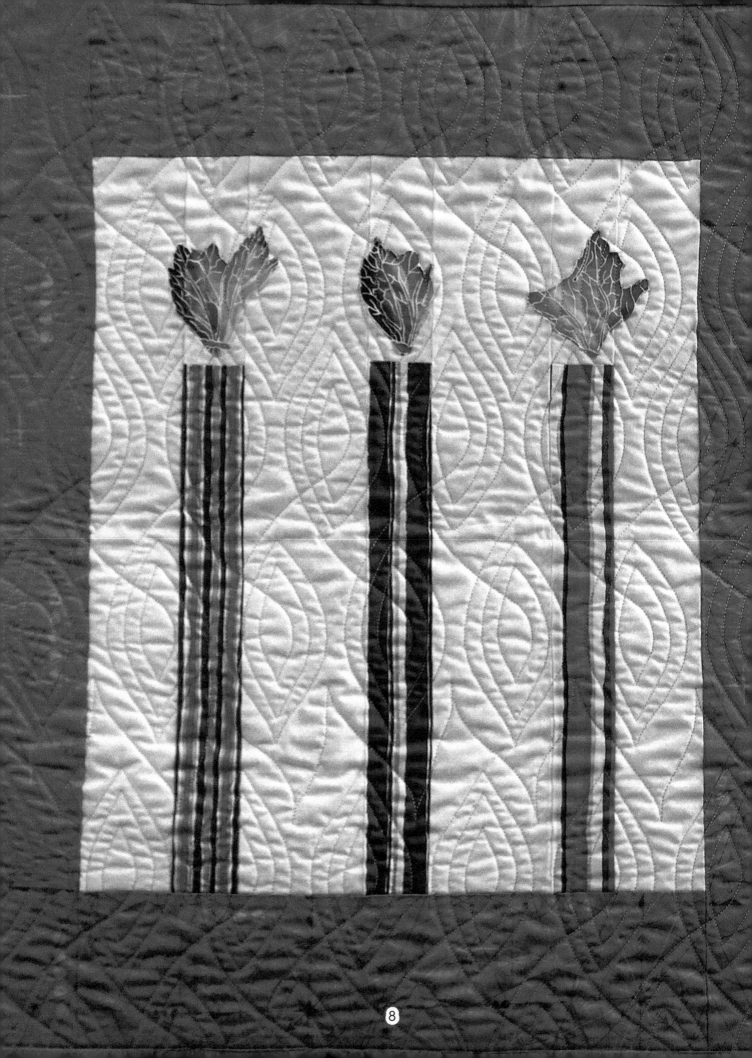

The Flame

a single spark is grace and power
it sees movements of the mind
it reflects emotions buried deep within

it's the tiny dancer
whirling rhythms of the heart
spinning a fire that burns

profound betrayal
twists and contorts in shadows
the flame defines darkness in her heart

her breath, once a sweet whisper
now angry, inhales sickness and disease
billows out an evil stench

without light
darkness and death rot the heart
toxic fumes spew out anger

hate ignites the wick
leaving my spirit
scorched and writhing in pain

my soul cries out

Pain, Too Painful

sometimes she cries when she's alone
deep in her soul she can still see their young faces

now that they're grown
she fears she wouldn't recognize them

she can't endure the agony
tears seep out, staining her cheeks

a heart broken and bent
shattered, aches from wounds

she screams from rage
shouts no one hears

sadness and anger are now her life
curse the gods!

she prays to see the children
time is running out

somebody help her
there is no one

they will be adults soon
she won't know them

will they know her?

A Child Starved of Love

dreams drowned in unending pain
tears define the destination
a path scorched in sorrows

unexpressed rage seethes
a soul painted burnt-black
cries tears of depression

a birthright of love never realized
a heart darkened
has no light...sees no sun

No One Asked

no one asked if their hearts were broken
no one asked what they had to say

oh, my sweet darlings
bitter foods were fed to you
they made you wince and cry

spit it out, I scream
your ears too far to hear

eat sweets to make you smile
hear my words
my will is to save you

an endless year not shared
I picture how you've grown

I search for you, you are so close...find me
imagine I hear you say
look, there's Granny!

I pray to hear you call my name

Healing

I Am Next to You

let the light within you
shine to keep you safe
never let it go out

to those who care for you
don't give them breath
to blow out your flame

they live in darkness
hate fills them with ice
souls too frozen for the sun to thaw

seek the healing sky
it is I who will lead your way
let my love guide your spirit

I am always next to you
my heart beats through yours
I live within your soul

my touch...my voice...my heart
I give to you

Can you still remember?

Always With Me

you're always with me...
you walk beside me
I hear your voice
I feel your heart beat

you are everywhere...
glow of the sun
scent of flowers
waves at the shore

you are the melody birds sing
joy in my heart
gift that gives me love

I pray to hear once more
you call on the phone and say
hi Granny, it's me!

Healing...Deserved
to be Loved

I was special
but no one knew

I had talent
but no one saw

I had beauty
but was neglected in *filth*

I had promise
but no support

I hated that little girl
always feeling less than

it took many years
before I was whole

I learned to become
my own best mother

to love myself
to believe in myself

embrace that little girl
who once was me...

cherish her
kiss her
dress her
love her

be her mother

The Yoga Posture...
The Warrior

I stand erect and grounded on my yoga mat
a sacred place to find healing
years of practice
lead me to this place

I step my feet wide apart
extend my winged arms, hands like pointed arrows
face right and turn my left foot in
as I bend towards my right hand
I gaze past my fingertips

looking behind me, is my past
sadness that stops my heart
I'm mindful to look forward
fix my sights to the future
visualize the possibilities

breathe...relax...stand strong
        be fierce
threaten away pain and sorrow
        be empowered

I soar, I sway
I'm an eagle gliding ...
wind teases my ears
sun pulls me close
senses satisfied

I am the warrior
of strength and grace
ablaze with passion
my heart is filled
a moment of peace...I am safe

Being in the Moment

tangled in a vacuous sphere
unknown to my present state
unspoken words speak to me
I am rubbed raw of thoughts

my vision disappears,
I am impaired by distractions
that bombard the complexities of life

I am not present...

I suffer the loss,
and search for self-involvement
in a relentless space
that blinds me

I have fought the struggle
to enjoy the passing of time,
but like a soft whisper
it has eluded me

I am not present...

I journey to find healing
urgent to raise my awareness
and transform sadness into peace
I am not present...

I have been gently guided by Yogis
to follow centuries' path of wisdom...
to breathe deeply within
to touch the core of my being

that breath centers me
its stillness transcends me,
I close my eyes to feel
my soul caress love

push thoughts of loss aside
feel touched by a wisp of wind
I can now hear the voices that speak

I feel I belong...

Enlightenment

sadness was sewn into the clothing she wore,
threaded into the depths of her brain.
she lived hidden in darkness, shame...*filth*

loneliness never soothed
wounds never healed
a lifetime of sorrow
she was a troubled soul

she craved affection
searched for safety
never knowing love
it came disguised as neglect.

she wouldn't let darkness define her

when life was too difficult to endure,
her mind took her to the ocean by the shore.
there waves rocked her like a mother's arms,
gently rolled over her like a lover

she found a haven in its calming rhythm
energy so strong and whirling,
it connected to her inner warrior

it was hidden strength that ignited
a more powerful force
to become the person
she wanted to be.

sadness would not defeat her

drawing her soul to the sun,
inhaling its energy
she was infused with joy

a state of bliss...became an addictive drug

centuries of people left footprints on the sand
for her to follow
she wanted to explore all she could
in a place where safety lived

her journey took her into darkness
where memory cells waited
for her to unleash

she begged for help

she waded in the ocean,
going deeper and still deeper
trying to tread water
drowning in awareness of her consciousness

colors exploded in her eyes,
afraid...voices spoke
a lifetime of questions answered

she wasn't prepared.
it took only a few minutes
to learn too much

her mind fragmented onto the shore

From Her Deck

it's the secrets
that still the soul
listening to melodies within
songbirds singing to her spirit

the canopy of trees above
sways beside breezes
it's the cradle
that soothes heat

for these moments...she is grateful

the woods shield her from pain
everything exists
to quiet a healing soul

a blanket of relief
covers her
promising safety
for today is peace

The Wedding Canopy

how could we have known
that a simple dance
would lead us to such enchantment

footsteps that took different paths
now walk side by side
share secrets of our souls

mosaic crystals of sand
made by our family
have joined brothers and sisters

bonds brought together
by our young grandchildren
connect cousins to a lifetime of love

beneath the flowered canopy we vow
we are to each other
the fulfillment of our needs

Love, Respect, Devotion

you are my home
you are my days
you are my life

The Open Window

she loves to watch the cats charge into the room
when they hear her open the window,
the sun's embracing vision shines complete

laying in the sun's warmth,
eyes squinting, deep in silent thoughts
Izzy and Vinny stand sentry for soaring birds.

Izzy, regal in his burnt orange coat
his cousin Vinny, purest of silver snow
both exquisite in their royal Siberian fur

sweet dreams bathe in the summer's kindness
sheltered in their right for contentment
free from neglect, safe in love

like a mother, she cares for them
sings to them when they walk into the room
gives them treats, the cousins purr in rhythm

watching them now
she is reminded of her childhood
wishes she had also been cherished

for a little girl...innocent of harm
shines love and protection
she craved for the child within her

they delight in her tenderness
a birthright she should have known
love in a mother's touch changes everything

No Sadness for Me

don't define me in darkness
don't define me in depression
don't define me in dejection

picture me instead, in blissful moments
see my heart smile in delight
think of me always in joyful pursuits

working in my garden
reading at the beach
watching sunrises
dancing to music
sewing at my machine
writing a poem

these interests I've enjoyed
lifted my spirits
filled my time with purpose

the greatest cure for sad spells
was holding you close to me
feeling your heart beat

you filled my being
as nothing else could
with your touch upon my soul

a life blessed with passion
a heart you filled with love
your song so sweet

Renewal

On The Day You Were Born

the sun painted rainbows that day
waves danced pirouettes on to the shore
sapphires bejeweled the sky in blues
on the day you were born

you are the essence of poise and strength
extraordinary in all you do
a voice sings the sweetness of your spirit
love of life radiates in your beauty

your gentle kindness
touches the heart of those captivated
warming lives in a blanket of grace
a light within you shining upon us all

I am overwhelmed with pride and joy
as you become a young woman
I am blessed you're my granddaughter
you are my sunshine and I celebrate you

I will love you always and forever...

Granny's Quilt

sleepovers are always the same
everything has to be perfect

the full pillow always in the same spot
upon the softest silk sheets
and of course, the fluffiest feather quilt
all wrapped up in lavish love

a squishy nightgown next is what she needs
swishing her hands
around swirls in the dresser drawer
she finds just the loveliest one

now, time to cuddle...

Noses touching
Sweet scents swimming
Spirits silently speaking
Souls searching

stratus clouds spin circles above their heads
brushes paint in pink and purple pastels
safety and love is forever
she finds comfort in her Granny's arms

she shares her secret in the sweet stillness
of monsters that come into her room at night.
"Oh no, there's no such thing."
"Oh yes, Granny, I've seen them."

her folded infant quilt
carefully put away years ago
sewn to sooth her newborn soft skin
is the answer now for a frightened child

Granny told her she had sewn a magic quilt
stitched with enchanted silk thread
just in case she needed it one day
to scare away monsters

even then, when she was so very tiny
she loved that quilt all scrunched up around her.
smiling, she'd squiggle and slide her skin
up and down the slippery slopes

she watches as Granny slips out of bed
to return with the quilt.
feeling it, the child aptly names it "Silky"
then forever more, its magic would stay by her side

Granny knew how to protect her
always had, always will

Granny's quilt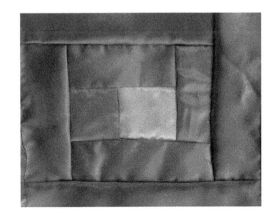

Coming of Age

Now that you're becoming a young woman
I feel the passage of time
for all the generations before you,
you are here...my shining star.

From the very first touch
you were so tender and warm
just to hold you and cradle you
filled me with peace.

Like the morning sunrise
you light my day with your laughter and smile
each day you give something to me
a gift that comes from just being you.

Your fingers dancing on the piano
with your sweet voice singing
fill my soul with song.

Your eyes see things in nature
that most never see
your heart is always reaching out.

Your goodness is seen through the joy you bring
looking at the world through your eyes
you show the beauties of life
and simple truths from which I've learned.

I feel the energy and love of my parents
being passed through me
and with all its power...
I pass it to you

The Woods...
Bryce Canyon

the forest stands to welcome its children.
underbrush carpet is a memory returned.

leaves embrace me
exotic heady fragrances comfort me

whooshing my feet through damp mire
I remember playing in piles of raked leaves, I smile

tall trees sway slightly
shed their golden leaves

gilded gems rain
to glisten my peaceful bliss

violins and sweet flutes
tell me stories of seasons passed

rustling plays a melody
songs of hope and security

branches keep me safe in their arms
here is where I want to be

I long to stay
my soul has come home

Dawn at Montauk

I rise and run east to the farthest point
dawn draws me to it

pinks and oranges singe the sky
brushes swirl, paint splashes

its brilliance is wild
cannot be captured

pastoral harmony sings for the soul
I am held in rapture

water colors flood my being
promising to paint possibilities...I dream

The Artist's Garden

luster of fresh paint
renders emerald gloss leaves
glorious scarlet geraniums
dawning daylilies
boisterous black-eyed daises

sweet scents of lavender:
saturate the air
soothe the mind
relax the senses
ignite thoughts
tell of mysteries

majestic butterflies flutter and float
delicate wings sway above
radiant flowers offer them love
splashes of colorful hues visit the garden
each day brings paintings of enchantment

Driving at Night

the woods greet me
embroidered hues of gray ombre
shaded by tangled branches
dance above

emotions float in the distance
folded across my chest, hands clenched
I am held in space
sharing the cosmos with my trees

deep inhalations
morph into mist
steam exhales into the chill
droplets drip...drip

the alarm sounds at dusk
eyes failing, I race home for safety
isolation suits only the lonely

You're Here with Me, Grand Canyon

I rush out of my cabin
in time to watch the sun spin twirls of pinks and purples

I sense you are here with me
at sunrise you both appear, your smiles bathed in light

giggles laugh among leaves
your hugs are the wind

the music of deep echoes
resonates against the canyon

bighorn sheep and mule deer roam freely
they appear for your delight

nothing compares to your tender heart
it shares secrets of your soul

together, your joyful eyes glimmer
within canyon walls.

the colors glow from within you
you are life...you two are my life!

When I Am Old

when I am old
birds will sing sweet songs
perched outside my window
fluffing and prancing for my delight
they will share secrets with me

when I am old
waves at the beach
will dance pirouettes onto the shore
they will cover me like a lover
and rock me in the surf

when I am old
the moon will hold me close
and draw my heart to it
the faces of the moon will light the night
and show me the way

when I am old
butterflies will visit to soothe me
a runway of unexpected divine hues
they will kiss the tops of my beloved garden
to bequeath their approval

when I am gone
my heart will fly with the love of my children
I will know their touch upon my wings
serenity will spill into my soul and I will smile
when I am gone

Fulfillment

Needles and Pins

the tapestry of my heart
a patchwork of intense colors
stitched with passion and love

quilts spun with golden threads
painted in loving hues
sewn to warm another's heart

intense amethyst
ignites passion's possibilities
in pinks and purples

blues, bejeweled in sapphires
tell the sweet intentions
adorned in one's heart

riotous reds, wild and rowdy
unspoiled to invite
a garden of emotions

imagine the possibilities
of people's pleasure
in royal majestic tones

treasures of simple squares and circles
sew the memories
in silks and satins

a profusion of colors
tell stories of friendship and love
from a simple stash of cloth

my heart's dream fulfilled
a life blessed
sewn into a mosaic of splendid pieces
I am grateful...

Magnificent Seven

a miraculous day ten years ago
started her heart beating again

grateful vision of a new grandbaby
filled her with hope for a new beginning

devastated by love once rejected years ago
she craved bonding with a new life

to her delight, one by one they were born
seven beating hearts to soothe a vacant soul

each one wiped a tear that had fallen
each one a cherub coming to heal her

tiny eyes spoke, assuring her of love
seven beating hearts to soothe a vacant soul

each born unique and extraordinary
they are...the magnificent seven

one by one, born in this order
1. compassionate
2. joyful
3. creative
4. bubbly
5. entertaining
6. spunky
7. loveable

they repaired her spirit...seven beating hearts to soothe
a vacant soul

Sadness

Jacenta Gonzalez

Dear Sad Person

Sincerely,
Violet

Original Book Cover
By: Gustings Vasco

Career Poem

When I grow up
What should I be?
A singer, a dancer
Or maybe an ice skater
Like Tara Lipinski

I'd be a fashion designer
And be on TV
Or maybe I could be
A general, a doctor
Or even an MC.

I'll be a famous scientist
And win a lot of awards
A waiter
A skater
Or maybe I can be in the
Army and fight in wars.

There is so much to do
So much to be
But hey, I have a lot of
Time to decide
So right now I'll just be
me!!
Bridget Sowulski

OUR OWN MYTHS

Why Wars Happen
Kevin Cardenas

Have Is a Tornado Formed?
Bridget Sowulski

Why We Have Snow
Raphael Martinez

Why We Have Dark Gray Clouds
Katy Rodriguez

Why We Have a Half Moon
Chrissy Bengel

Daysi Merino

Why Being Brother
Katherine King

As the sun set, the sky was flooded with colors
My heart shattered into a million pieces as leaves cartwheeled to the ground
Christina Bonal

The sun is the light from the heavens
Christina Bonal

Shealie Vazquez

Why We Have Snow
Ilena Hernandez

Sad
Alone
Pamella Wong

Rainy days, signs of winter whispering through the air
Maurice Green

The sea was as bright as the sky on a sunny summer's day
Jeancarlos Cestin

The snow is like a white blanket covering the South Pole
Jeancarlos Cestin

What Should I Be?
Benjamin Filancini

January Blues

Christmas is over
No more Christmas cheer
So children pack your bags
Cause school is here
A year has passed
without a trace
Cause 1999
Has won the race
Christina Bonal

MY NAME IS OSCAR

"Hello! My name is Oscar. I live in your house somewhere. Sometimes I will follow you and you know I am there. You will not look behind you, you will just walk slowly when you feel my presence. You know who you are. When you come up the stairs you tend to run. Do you know who you are now? I am with you in the darkness of your home and make you feel creepy. Most of all you won't admit that you are scared by my presence but you are and you will jump in your little bed and cover your head with the cover thinking I won't follow you. But I am always beside you in the dark so remember my little ones, you are being followed in the dark by Oscar.

By: Madeline Tropiano

A Flock Of Feelings
A Thanksgiving Poem

Indian Picking Berries
A Thanksgiving Poem
Cynthia Andujar

A Flock Of Poems

November
Kavita Wessard

November
Jaceta Gonzalez

January Poem

Bouquet of Feelings
Benjamin Filancini

I'd Like School To Be...
By: Sergio Soto

November Days
On every tree
Leaves turn colors
Maurice Green

Why We ...
Richard Olivera

Career Poems

What Will I Be?

What Should I Be?

My Future Career

What Should I Be?

THE DOLL
Christina Singel

HALLOWEEN

Halloween is spooky,
Trick or treating
On Halloween
Seeing witches
Ghosts and goblins
Makes me want to scream.
The scary monsters
Makes me want to shake.
All around me
Are costumes
When I finally awake
Jackie Celio

My Future Career

Principals, accountants, teachers, too
So much to be, so much to do
What should I be?
Pamella Wong

Literature Everywhere
By Pamella Wong

Happiness

When you want to be happy
Happiness is ...
Katy Rodriques

THE HAUNTED HOUSE

On October 31st at midnight the witches cast their spells on people. That night I went trick- or -treating with my brother. We saw the house the witches lived in. The house had a black cat next to the door. The cat had yellow eyes and was black all over. The house was covered with spider webs including the trees. My brother and I did not want to go up to the door and ask for candy. We walked very fast past this spooky looking house. We walked around the other streets getting bags full of candy. We never saw that house again!

KAVITA PERSHAD

Our Monthly Poems

Thanksgiving

Happy Thanksgiving
Madeline Tropiano

January
Sergio Soto

December
Michael Gonzales

Simon Sez

Feelings
Feelings, feelings
Everywhere ...
There's sadness
Anger and fear
Michael Gonzales

Dear Olga

Happy And Sad
When I am happy ...
Shealie Vazquez

Christmas Day
Violet Dubrovsky

Halloween
Witch witch
On a broom stick

Flock of Feelings
When school starts
Daysi Merino

November
Brian Diaz

Jobs
What will I do?
So many jobs
Brian Diaz

With Gratitude

hundreds of students gladdened my heart
filled my classroom with joy and love

each with hidden talents
possibilities I guided them to reveal

what a delight watching them evolve
my sixth graders coming to life in new ways

each child seeking approval
I showed them the way

written on the board every morning
a journal topic to ponder and share

secrets hidden inside
divulged and discussed

no judgements made
our classroom became a safe haven

Peter cried when he said
kids in class always make fun of him

one by one they confessed...apologized
remorseful for being cruel

so proud of these special moments
I helped children feel accepted

I inspired them to realize their capability
they in turn, made me aware of my impact

over thirty years spent doing what I loved
a lifetime of fulfillment

a career designed, suited for my needs
so fortunate...so grateful

Her Garden

it's a faint whisper
she strains to hear,
trees speak of breezes
a harmony of soft rustling

everything listens

songbirds sing sweet refrains to the heart
they stop and say prayers
the joy in the symphony
embraces her soul

her garden porch is the secret
a tranquil space
private thoughts
a gift to her senses

the wind's breath
scatters seeds of fresh paint...

glossy greens
goldenrods of deep yellow
gracious gladiolus
glorious crimson geraniums
golden daylilies
grand scent of lavender perfume

all drift into her soul...a pastoral trance

simplicity of moments
swirl in her being
sustain her mind
assign peace within

EVERYONE HAS A FRIEND

Best Friends

DURING EACH STAGE
OF LIFE

THE LUCKY ONES HAVE
THE SAME FRIEND IN
ALL STAGES OF LIFE...

A BFF

While we were children
growing up
we found one another
to love, to trust

At so young an age
we cared for each other
making a bond
to be there for the other

It was always so simple,
you and I
to share our thoughts
held deep inside

My feelings you hold
no one else can touch
for a lifetime of love
flowers the seeds of trust

Keeping Traditions

a lifetime ago in a tiny kitchen
   stands my Mom and Aunt Harriet
      cooking a holiday dinner...I am ten

it's steaming with heat
   no air conditioners then
      I scribble on dewy windows

sweat pours down their noses
   drip...drip...onto food-stained housedresses
      ones saved for cooking

my cousin, Ingrid and I stand in the doorway
   no room for us all to fit inside
      we are hysterical watching them

once again they try to make the potato casserole
   either it comes out greyish green and tastes delicious
      or looks golden brown and is dreadful

one more time they burn the sautéed onions
　　this makes them tear up with laughter
　　　　using the extra onions, they keep trying

my cousin and I peek in...to watch...to learn
　　dream of our turn to sauté onions and to sweat
　　　　for our someday family to be

fast forward, I am standing in my kitchen
　　cooking the holiday dinner
　　　　air conditioner keeping me cool

our families are too many to share dinners now
　　we always said we'd cook together, never did
　　　　instead, we cook on the phone and laugh

sautéing onions, I hear Mom and Aunt Harriet
　　they are next to me, showing me the way
　　　　helping me keep family traditions to pass on

A Life Lived

wished on stars for promises
so thankful I was given it all
dreams...always lighting passion

in the mirror of my life
with too few breaths left
a reflection shines upon much

music played a narrative of the years
the decades danced in romantic steps
syncopated rhythms swayed in tune

I was the joyful spirit twirling at the party
listening to songs, spinning in music
arms stretched out waiting for the dance

I have been touched by the sun
immersed in flowers
nature whispering enchantments, in step beside me

the moon held me close
drawing my heart to it
faces lit the night and showed me the way

waves hugged the beach
to rock and caress me
embracing warmth upon my soul

birds visited to sing their songs
telling their secrets of hope
between the beating of their wings

I have been touched by hundreds of children
sitting at desks, filling my days...and years
their lessons always of the giving heart

divine touch of my babies
their sweetness in simple smiles
tiny fingers on my skin...my soul sang

the Yogis' practice of deep inhalations
centered my core, protected me
from life's often painful truths

they say...a life isn't measured in breaths,
but the moments that take your breath away
I am filled with the joy of moments

About The Author

Leslie is a published poet and retired New York City elementary school teacher. She's had a fulfilling career integrating her love of poetry into her classroom, received many awards for outstanding teaching and was published in the New York State Curriculum Guide, and New York State Exemplary Teachers.

Along with poetry writing, designing quilts is her life's passion. Her quilts tell stories and illuminate emotions of her poems.

Recently remarried, she and her husband share a blended family of grandkids, sisters and brothers-in-law. Being a Grandmother brings her boundless joy. She's traveled to countries she always dreamed of visiting. Eating was the highlight of her trips... croissants in Paris, pizza in Italy, baklava in Greece, basically ate her way through every country.

Family and good friends fill her life with gratitude.

Readers can reach Leslie Simon at sewpoetic@aol.com

CPSIA information can be obtained
at www.ICGtesting.com
Printed in the USA
BVHW090716281020
591938BV00002B/18